REBEL GIRLS

LEVEL UP

25 TALES OF GAMING AND THE METAVERSE

Good Night Stories for Rebel Girls and Rebel Girls are registered trademarks.
Good Night Stories for Rebel Girls and all other Rebel Girls titles are available for bulk purchase for sale promotions, premiums, fundraising, and educational needs.
For details, write to sales@rebelgirls.com.

This is a work of creative nonfiction. It is a collection of heartwarming and thought-provoking stories inspired by the lives and adventures of 25 influential women. It is not an encyclopedic account of the events and accomplishments of their lives.

www.rebelgirls.com

Some of the artwork in this book has been previously published in the book *Good Night Stories for Rebel Girls: 100 Real-Life Tales of Black Girl Magic*.

Library of Congress Control Number: 2022948130
Rebel Girls, Inc.
421 Elm Ave.
Larkspur, CA 94939

Text by Jenelle Swan, Emma Carlson Berne, and Eliza Kirby
Art direction by Giulia Flamini
Cover illustrations by Annalisa Ventura
Graphic design by Kristen Brittain
Special thanks: Cordia Leung, Erin McDearman, Grace Srinivasiah, Jacob Roach, Jes Wolfe, Maithy Vu, Marina Asenjo, Mindy Jafek, Neha Narang

Printed in China, 2023
10 9 8 7 6 5 4 3 2 1
ISBN: 978-1-953424-46-4

FSC
www.fsc.org
MIX
Paper | Supporting
responsible forestry
FSC™ C018179

CONTENTS

FOREWORD BY ELIZA KIRBY   4

AMBER ALLEN • CEO   6
AMIRA VIRGIL • Creator and Community Builder   8
AMY HENNIG • Director and Script Writer   10
ANNE SHOEMAKER • Game Designer   12
AYA KYOGOKU • Director and Producer   14
BRITTNEY MORRIS • Video Game Writer and Novelist   16
CATHY HACKL • Business Executive and Tech Futurist   18
CSAPPHIRE • Digital Clothing Designer   20
FELICIA DAY • Actor, Creator, and Streamer   22
HELEN CHIANG • Video Game Studio Head   24
IHASCUPQUAKE • Streamer and Influencer   26
JAY-ANN LOPEZ • Community Builder, CEO, and Founder   28
JENNIFER TOWNE • Environment and 3D Artist   30
KELLEE SANTIAGO • Game Designer, Producer, and Founder   32
MACKENSEIZE • Streamer   34
MADDIE MESSER • Gamer   36
MANAMI MATSUMAE • Composer   38
MARINA DÍEZ PEREIRO • Game Developer   40
MURIEL TRAMIS • Game Designer   42
PHOEBE WATSON • Game Designer   44
POKIMANE • Streamer   46
POORNIMA SEETHARAMAN • Game Designer   48
SASHA HOSTYN • Esports Player   50
SHELLY MAZZANOBLE • Gamer and Podcaster   52
SYLVIA GATHONI • Esports Player   54

WRITE YOUR STORY   56
DRAW YOUR PORTRAIT   57
KEEP PLAYING!   58
A NOTE ON ILLUSTRATIONS   61
THE ILLUSTRATORS   63
ABOUT REBEL GIRLS   64

FOREWORD

Hi Rebels,

When I was a kid, I loved computer games. I'd build elaborate theme parks in *Roller Coaster Tycoon* and create families in *The Sims* that I kept going for generations. My best friend and I would play the third *Harry Potter* game together, with one of us using the keyboard to control where Harry or Hermione walked and the other using the mouse to control their wand. Even though I'd sit at the computer in my family's basement until my eyes itched and it was dark outside, I didn't really think of myself as a gamer. My brother, though—*he* was a gamer. He played sports games and action adventures on PlayStation. To me, that seemed like the "right" way to be a gamer—playing on a console, and playing as a boy.

When I started working on this book, I did a lot of research on gaming and tech, and I realized how much of the gaming world is geared toward boys and away from girls. And when you look at the teams behind a lot of games, you start to see one reason: there are not many women in this industry. I can't tell you how many times I looked up a popular video game and scrolled through the developers, directors, writers, artists, and producers, only to see male name after male name listed. Why were there so few women in this world? Why was it possible for entire games to be made without the involvement of a single woman? And what did that mean for the games themselves? What did it mean for all of the girls and women out there playing them?

According to some surveys, women make up 48 percent of gamers in the United States and 40 to 45 percent of gamers in Asia. Yet only 24 percent of people working in gaming are women. At the highest levels, a whopping 84 percent of positions are held by men. And when you look at the games themselves, the numbers get even more discouraging—only 5 percent of video games feature female main characters.

It's easy to get frustrated about this. I know I did! But reading about the amazing accomplishments of the women who work in this industry gave me hope for the future of gaming.

Rebel Girls Level Up features the stories of 25 inspiring women who are involved in gaming and tech at every level. You'll meet some of the high-powered women behind your favorite games, like Helen Chiang, studio head at *Minecraft*, and Aya Kyogoku, director of several *Animal Crossing* games. You'll read about community builders like Jay-Ann Lopez, who work to make gaming a more inclusive place. You'll feel like you're watching streamers and professional gamers like Pokimane and Sasha Hostyn, who redefined what it means to be a gamer girl. And you'll get to know some of the newest faces in the industry, like Jennifer Towne, cSapphire, and Anne Shoemaker, who are creating incredible gaming experiences on Roblox.

I hope these stories inspire you to explore the wide world of gaming and get you excited about all the incredible innovations the future has in store. Know that however you like to game, you're a gamer—just like the Rebel Girls in this book.

—Eliza Kirby, Editor, Rebel Girls

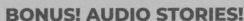

BONUS! AUDIO STORIES!

Download the Rebel Girls app to hear longer stories about some of the impactful creators and leaders in this book. You will also find engaging activities and discover stories of other trailblazing women. Whenever you come across a star icon, scan the code, and you'll be whisked away on an audio adventure.

SCAN TO HEAR MORE!

AMBER ALLEN

CEO

Once upon a time, a gamer girl in east Texas played all the video games she could get her hands on. She played *Mortal Kombat* at home. She played arcade games at Pizza Hut. She played *Super Mario Bros.*, *Halo*, and *The Legend of Zelda*. Her name was Amber, and games were her way of being with people. She would play with her friends and with her brother. Together, they could be creative.

As Amber got older, her curiosity kept her moving, exploring new ways to create. She was fascinated by technology and all the cool developments it brought to gaming. When she was a grown-up, she learned about an exciting online space called the "metaverse." In the metaverse, people could explore interesting places, learn new skills, and meet up with their friends—all without ever leaving home. Amber wanted to be right at the front of this fascinating world.

Later, Amber started her own metaverse company, Double A Labs. Double A helps create digital worlds where people can work together. One of Amber's clients wanted to educate people about space-travel safety. So Double A Labs helped them build a gaming experience that makes people feel like they're on a space shuttle. Using what she learned as a gamer, Amber helps create technologies that teach people new things. She knows that if you're having fun, you'll learn more!

Amber still loves video games. She even has a whole gaming room in her house. She loves to play with people who come over. It's like being back in Texas, playing games with her brother and her friends. They're having fun, being creative, and, most important, connecting with one another.

BORN APRIL 22
UNITED STATES OF AMERICA

"EVERY DAY THAT
CHILDHOOD AMBER
HIGH-FIVES ADULT
AMBER, I WIN."
—AMBER ALLEN

AMIRA VIRGIL

CREATOR AND COMMUNITY BUILDER

Amira grinned as she sorted through all the different outfits in *The Sims*. There were bright-blue dresses, business clothes, and even fantasy costumes. But when she went to pick her character's skin tone, she paused, cursor hovering over the few options. The game had no dark skin colors that matched her own.

Maybe it'll be better in the next game in the series, Amira thought. But the same thing happened each time she booted up the newest version of *The Sims*. She could customize everything from ear size to eye color—but the skin tones still didn't look like hers. Amira couldn't believe it. She could create a more realistic alien avatar than a character of herself!

By the time *The Sims 4* came out, Amira was making mods of her own. These downloaded content packs allowed other players to install more options for skin tones and hairstyles into their own *Sims* games. Players around the world loved how realistic Amira's mods made their avatars look.

Amira had also become a streamer, someone who broadcasts videos of themselves playing games. On her channel, she spoke out about the lack of skin color options. Amira was glad her mods were successful, but she felt like they shouldn't be needed at all. Why couldn't the game developers just make games that represented the way people looked in the real world?

The creators of *The Sims* heard her—and to her surprise, they agreed. The company announced they would release diverse content to *The Sims 4*. Every time Amira logs in, she can see how her actions have changed the world—and countless digital worlds too!

BORN OCTOBER 4, 1994
UNITED STATES OF AMERICA

"IT'S IMPORTANT . . . THAT THESE COMPANIES DO RIGHT BY THE MARGINALIZED COMMUNITIES THAT THEY TRY TO INCLUDE BY ACTUALLY INCLUDING THEM."
—AMIRA VIRGIL

ILLUSTRATION BY SHIRLEY HOTTIER

AMY HENNIG

DIRECTOR AND SCRIPT WRITER

Once upon a time, there was a girl whose head was filled with stories. At first, Amy thought she wanted to work in the film industry. But after college, she wasn't sure it was the right way to tell the tales brewing in her mind.

Instead, Amy got a job as an artist on a game called *Electrocop*. Though *Electrocop* would never release, Amy found that she loved building trees, monsters, and cities. She made settings that looked like you could step right into them. It was almost like creating the backgrounds for a movie!

Right away, though, Amy realized that her job wouldn't be easy. Every time she finished a project, she had to keep interviewing for places on development teams. The first game she worked on after *Electrocop* was canceled, and the games that followed lacked the fantasy adventures she wanted to build.

After many years of hard work, Amy got a job on a series called *Uncharted*. She'd be in charge of the whole story! She wrote four games about a man named Nathan Drake and his scary, action-packed adventures.

When she finished working on *Uncharted*, Amy decided she wanted to create her own games. At her new company, she focused on games with sweeping stories and complicated characters. She wanted players to feel excited as they explored mysteries and uncovered new worlds.

Although Amy left her movie dreams behind to work on video games, she has brought her two interests together, creating games for film series like Star Wars. She has become a powerful leader who can take charge of the projects she loves, bringing the stories in her head to life.

BORN AUGUST 19, 1964
UNITED STATES OF AMERICA

"WE WANT OUR CHARACTERS TO BE COMPLEX AND FLAWED AND INTERESTING AND LAYERED."
—AMY HENNIG

CREATED USING
AI ILLUSTRATION

ANNE SHOEMAKER

GAME DESIGNER

Anne has always been an artist. When she was a little kid, she would paint using her computer. She liked watching the pixels change color as she clicked her mouse, creating beautiful pictures on the screen. But she wanted more—she wanted to see her art move! Anne learned to do simple animations and made up stories to go along with them. *When I grow up*, Anne told herself, *I'm going to work in a movie animation studio.*

Then Anne started playing on the gaming platform Roblox. There, she could make up even more stories. But not everyone thought video games were as fantastic as Anne did. *Stop letting Anne play those games*, other grown-ups would tell her mom. *She's wasting her time!*

Anne disagreed. She disagreed so much that when she was a young adult, she started teaching herself how to make video games. She had to learn how to code and design and do 3D modeling.

It was hard, but Anne did learn. She started making up and designing games for Roblox. Her games got so popular that she hired people to help her. This was a new challenge—now Anne wasn't just an artist on her own. She was a boss and a leader. If she had an idea for a new video game, she had to explain it to her artists. She had to help the whole team make the game together.

"I love the idea of spending your time going toward things that make you happy," Anne said. Designing video games makes her happy, just like making art did when she was little. But now, she doesn't have to keep her digital creations on her computer—the whole world can enjoy them.

BORN AUGUST 20, 1999
UNITED STATES OF AMERICA

"THE METAVERSE IS JUST A VIRTUAL SPACE TO EXPERIENCE ANYTHING YOU CAN IMAGINE WITH YOUR FRIENDS . . . YOU WANT TO FLY? YOU CAN FLY. YOU WANT TO BE A MERMAID? YOU CAN BE A MERMAID!"
—ANNE SHOEMAKER

AYA KYOGOKU

DIRECTOR AND PRODUCER

Aya walked up the steps of Nintendo in 2003, feeling excited but nervous. It was her big dream to work at the well-known gaming company. But she knew she would be one of the few women working there.

At first, Aya struggled. She wrote the scripts for games like *The Legend of Zelda: Four Swords Adventures* and *Twilight Princess*, planning out adventurous stories about Link and Princess Zelda. Sadly, it wasn't uncommon for Aya to be the only woman on a team, and her ideas for male characters like Link were often ignored. She would sit at her desk, working out dialogue, feeling frustrated.

So many games are made with boys in mind, she thought, *when girls like me love them just as much*. There had to be a way to work on a project where people would listen to her ideas.

One day, Aya heard about a new project for a popular game series. The company that made *Animal Crossing* wanted to bring equal numbers of male and female creators together to make a more diverse and inclusive game. Aya was offered the opportunity to join the team!

As the director, she encouraged her teammates to share their ideas and create vivid and compelling characters. Aya made sure no one felt left out.

Animal Crossing: City Folk was a huge success. Players loved building their own towns and meeting unique characters. Aya kept working on more versions of *Animal Crossing*. Eventually, she became the person who creates the ideas for new video games. She was the first woman to hold that post for Nintendo. Aya knows speaking out and taking risks can help create a more inclusive world—and that's exactly what she's doing.

BORN JANUARY 21, 1981
JAPAN

ILLUSTRATION BY
MARCELA RODRIGUEZ

"WHEN THERE ARE WOMEN
IN A VARIETY OF ROLES ON
THE PROJECT, YOU GET A
WIDER [RANGE] OF IDEAS."
—AYA KYOGOKU

BRITTNEY MORRIS

VIDEO GAME WRITER AND NOVELIST

Brittney sat in the theater, popcorn bucket forgotten in her lap as her gaze remained fixed on the credits rolling across the screen. Even though the movie was over, her heart was still racing from *Black Panther*'s action-packed fights. The setting—a beautiful, bountiful country filled with powerful Black characters—was a place she wanted to escape to.

I wonder if I could write something like that? she mused.

Black Panther stuck with Brittney. It explored real-life issues, like racism, in a vibrant fantasy world. She loved video games, and she wanted to write a book that tackled these same issues in gaming. She began drafting a story about a young developer who brings her experiences as a Black girl gamer into the game she is building.

Brittney's book *SLAY* was the first of many novels she would write. Her characters figure out how to stand up for themselves, both online and in person. They learn to love who they are and celebrate their differences.

As Brittney published books about the real-world experiences of Black teenagers, she also wrote novels set in video game worlds. Working with Insomniac Games, she wrote the book *Marvel's Spider-Man: Miles Morales—Wings of Fury*. Brittney realized Miles's story was similar to *SLAY*. He battled prejudice in his daily life while also fighting crime as Spider-Man.

Insomniac Games was impressed with Brittney's work. They asked her to help write *Marvel's Spider-Man 2* for PS5. Now she wasn't just writing about video games—she was writing the games themselves! As Miles slides on his mask and slings webs high above New York City, he'll have Brittney and her team's powerful storytelling propelling him forward.

BORN MARCH 24, 1991
UNITED STATES OF AMERICA

ILLUSTRATION BY
LYDIA MBA

"SOCIETAL EXPECTATIONS
OFTEN STEM FROM
STEREOTYPES. DON'T BE
AFRAID TO NOT FIT THEM."
—BRITTNEY MORRIS

CATHY HACKL

BUSINESS EXECUTIVE AND TECH FUTURIST

SCAN TO HEAR MORE!

Once upon a time, there was a girl named Cathy who liked to play video games, but she never called herself a gamer. *Gaming is for boys*, people said. *Is that true?* Cathy wondered. She loved the stories and the worlds in her video games. *Why can't I be a gamer too?*

Later, Cathy started working in the world of tech. All around her, she saw men in positions of power. Cathy was a woman, and she was Latina. No one looked like her. But Cathy wasn't going to apologize for who she was. She was going to speak loudly about her work and create a space for herself.

Cathy decided to mash up her two loves: tech and storytelling. She wanted to work in the metaverse, a place where physical and virtual worlds come together. Cathy knew that the metaverse could help people travel, experience events, and express themselves without the limits of the real world. She started producing all kinds of virtual experiences.

When Cathy produces virtual concerts, an avatar of the performer is projected onto a virtual stage in a virtual arena. Avatars of fans fill the virtual audience. The camera moves as the performers sing and dance, making fans feel as if they're really there, rocking out to the music. Cathy can create concerts with the most famous singers and bands—something she couldn't do if the concerts were in the real world.

Cathy loves working in the metaverse. "I want to be a beacon of hope for women in tech," she says. She invests money in companies led by women and creates scholarships for women who want to go into tech. Soon, there will be more and more Cathys in tech because she was willing to be one of the first.

BORN MAY 5
UNITED STATES OF AMERICA AND COSTA RICA

"I DECIDED TO TAKE A PAGE OUT OF MY MALE COUNTERPARTS' BOOKS AND RUN WITH THAT."
—CATHY HACKL

ILLUSTRATION BY GIULIA PIRAS

CSAPPHIRE

DIGITAL CLOTHING DESIGNER

SCAN TO HEAR MORE!

Once upon a time, there was a girl named Kyasia who loved fashion and video games. She especially liked playing dress-up video games on her computer. When she was seven, Kyasia saw an ad for Roblox. In the Roblox world, players could make avatars, or digital versions of themselves, and hang out with one another. It looked like fun. Kyasia started playing. She would dress up her avatar in different clothes.

But soon, Kyasia felt frustrated. She wanted to dress her avatar in clothes she'd wear in real life. But as she scrolled through outfit options, she didn't see anything she liked. She decided to fix that problem—herself.

When she was 12, Kyasia started designing her own virtual clothes for Roblox avatars. She called herself cSapphire. But since she was one of the first people to try to be a Roblox fashion designer, no one could teach her. So cSapphire was her own teacher. It could be challenging, but she felt proud that no one else had made designs like hers before.

After a while, cSapphire thought she'd see if players would want to buy her designs for their own avatars. Yes! They did! More than 600,000 people bought one of her earliest designs. cSapphire created ripped jeans, sparkly tank tops, and pink sweaters printed with hearts. These clothes were just like things she'd wear in her own life.

Real-life fashion designers noticed cSapphire's work. In 2021, she won the Fashion Award for Metaverse Design, given out by the British Fashion Council. Before this, these awards had only celebrated real-world clothes. "This was the first time they ever gave out this award," cSapphire said. "And I earned it just by creating clothes on Roblox!"

BORN AUGUST 31, 2001
UNITED STATES OF AMERICA

ILLUSTRATION BY
TALIA SKYLES

"WHAT I LOVE MOST ABOUT . . .
THE METAVERSE IS THAT PEOPLE
ARE ABLE TO EXPRESS THEMSELVES
IN ANY WAY POSSIBLE."
—CSAPPHIRE

FELICIA DAY

ACTOR, CREATOR, AND STREAMER

Once upon a time, a little girl scored the part of Scout in a local production of *To Kill a Mockingbird*. Felicia fell in love with the bright lights on the stage, the dusty smell of props, and the joy of telling a story. She knew she was destined to be an actor.

Felicia had a tough time getting into plays. She and her brother were both homeschooled, so she couldn't volunteer for class productions or audition for roles in the high school theater. Instead, she studied the violin and spent her free time playing classic video games filled with epic fantasy adventures.

After years of practice, Felicia went to college on a violin scholarship. Many of her classmates focused on just one subject, but not Felicia. She studied science, practiced violin, acted in plays, and danced onstage. And after all that, she still found time to play her fantasy-themed video games!

Felicia acted in a few TV shows, but she hadn't gotten the chance to tell her own story. One day, she settled in with her computer and began writing. She transformed her love of gaming into *The Guild*, a web show about a gamer girl who goes on a wild adventure with friends she meets while playing. Millions of people tuned in. Felicia realized that people everywhere connected with her journey.

Felicia keeps reaching out to fans in different ways. On her Twitch channel, she shares playthroughs of games while eating snacks, wearing wigs, and singing funny songs. She wants to make sure the gaming world is open and welcoming to as many people as possible. By sharing her story, she's shown that there's not just one way to be a gamer.

BORN JUNE 28, 1979
UNITED STATES OF AMERICA

ILLUSTRATION BY
JULIETTE TOMA

"I LOVE CREATING
COMMUNITIES
IN WHICH
PEOPLE CAN BE
THEMSELVES."
—FELICIA DAY

HELEN CHIANG

VIDEO GAME STUDIO HEAD

Nervous and excited, Helen stood in front of the camera, ready to film a video that would show *Minecraft* players around the world what was coming next for the game. She had just become the head of *Minecraft*. She knew it was going to be a big job, and it all started with talking to the most important part of the game: the players.

Even though she grew up playing video games with her little brother, Helen didn't realize she could actually *work* on games. After learning all she could about engineering, computer science, and business, she eventually started working for Xbox. There, Helen was struck by the incredible community that gaming created. It didn't matter who a gamer was or where they lived—they could log into a game and instantly connect with people they would never have met otherwise.

As the head of *Minecraft*, Helen was determined to make the best experiences possible for all its players. If you're playing *Minecraft* on a Nintendo Switch, you have Helen to thank for that! And if you've ever marveled at an axolotl, an underwater salamander, swimming through a *Minecraft* cave, that was Helen's doing too.

While Helen spends long hours creating updates for *Minecraft*, she also works with Girls Make Games, a program of camps and workshops that teach girls to make their own games. She knows there are thousands of girls playing *Minecraft* who could grow up to design the games of the future.

Helen hopes that young girls will see her work and know that gaming doesn't just have to be a hobby. It can be a career—and any woman who puts her mind to it can rise up and be a leader.

BIRTH DATE UNKNOWN

UNITED STATES OF AMERICA

"I LOVE THAT *MINECRAFT* CAN UNLOCK THAT CREATIVITY IN PEOPLE AND REALLY GIVE THEM THE OPPORTUNITY TO BUILD A LIFE FOR THEMSELVES ON IT."
—HELEN CHIANG

ILLUSTRATION BY BEA BARROS

IHASCUPQUAKE

STREAMER AND INFLUENCER

Tiffany perched on the edge of her bed and faced her laptop screen. The little green light told her the camera was on. She was ready to record. She opened up her current video game and filmed herself as she played and talked. Tiffany's setup wasn't great. She didn't even have a desk in her room to put the laptop on!

For her screen name, Tiffany chose iHasCupquake. She didn't really have a plan for her videos. At first, she focused on game playthroughs. Lots of people left comments cheering her on and sharing their thoughts. But she filmed herself doing regular things too, like making cake pops for her college graduation party. When she put that video on YouTube, it got tons of views. So Tiffany started making more baking videos.

Tiffany's videos got more and more popular. People commented on them, saying what they liked and didn't like. *You have the best laugh!* one person might say. Tiffany had a connection with her commenters. She loved being supported by her fans and feeling like she had created a community.

Soon, Tiffany decided to become a full-time online streamer and influencer. She got a microphone and a computer desk. For her college graduation gift, her parents gave her a desktop computer. Finally, Tiffany's videos had a sleek, polished look.

Tiffany was getting tired of working all day and long into the night, though. Sometimes, she read so many comments on her posts that she didn't know what she thought of things. Tiffany decided to post a little less. That was okay with Tiffany's followers. Her YouTube channel had 5 million subscribers. Tiffany's influence wasn't going anywhere.

BORN MARCH 19, 1988
UNITED STATES OF AMERICA

"I NEED TO CREATE MY FUTURE NOW . . . I NEED TO STOP WAITING. IT'S NOT GOING TO HAPPEN UNLESS I DO SOMETHING ABOUT IT."
—IHASCUPQUAKE

ILLUSTRATION BY SONIA LAZO

JAY-ANN LOPEZ

COMMUNITY BUILDER, CEO, AND FOUNDER

SCAN TO HEAR MORE!

Once upon a time, a woman with great style and a love for video games wanted to see more people like her online. Jay-Ann would often sit at her computer watching videos of gamers and streamers, but she noticed that few Black women popped up on her feeds. The harder she searched, the more upset she became. *Why aren't more women like me sharing their gaming experiences?* Jay-Ann wondered.

Jay-Ann began to research. The problem wasn't that there were no Black women in gaming. There were a lot of women like her! But many of them were afraid to tell their stories. The gaming world was not always kind to Black women. Sometimes, streamers would make fun of Black speech, hair, and culture. Some Black girl gamers got hateful emails or mean comments on videos. These horrible attacks made them feel scared and unsafe. Reading each story broke Jay-Ann's heart.

Slamming her hands down on her desk, she shook her head. *This has to change!* she said. So Jay-Ann created Black Girl Gamers, a Facebook page where Black women with a passion for gaming could celebrate their diverse ideas in a safe space. Jay-Ann watched in awe as the group grew, swelling from just a few tentative gamers to thousands of powerful voices.

Jay-Ann turned her Facebook group into a website committed to promoting diversity in every aspect of gaming. She is determined to see more Black women not just as streamers on Twitch or YouTube, but as leaders in game development. Whatever she does, Jay-Ann makes space for Black girl gamers. Together, she and her community can talk about what they love without fear.

BORN FEBRUARY 21
UNITED KINGDOM

"STAND OUT IN YOUR
UNIQUENESS."
—JAY-ANN LOPEZ

JENNIFER TOWNE

ENVIRONMENT AND 3D ARTIST

Once upon a time, there was a little girl who loved building worlds with Legos. Jenny would sit at her desk, in front of an empty Lego base, and start creating. She'd stack the little plastic blocks higher and higher, watching multicolored towers and castles grow before her eyes. She'd make up characters and stories to go with her buildings. Later, Jenny started playing on Roblox. *Like Legos on a screen*, she thought. She could make up her own world there too.

On Roblox, Jenny started designing environments—rooms and landscapes for characters to live in. One of her first Roblox projects was a mossy bridge. But the parts on the screen wouldn't stay where she wanted. She didn't want to ask for help. Big mistake, Jenny learned. Other developers could have shown her how to do it. Instead, Jenny struggled until she figured it out herself.

Under the name JennyBean, she kept creating environments. Some of them didn't work out—a volcano, Jenny's dream house, Jenny's *real* house. But that was okay. Jenny knew that trying new things was part of being an artist.

One day, Jenny started an environment of a medieval blacksmith's shop for a game called *Tranquility*. It was the first environment she had created in 3D. But Jenny couldn't figure out how she wanted it to look. Her creativity was blocked.

Tranquility sat on Jenny's computer for four months. One day, she had an idea. An image of swords before a roaring fire came into her head. She drew them, watching as the setting came to life. Jenny was proud of *Tranquility*. The little girl who played with Legos had made a whole world.

BORN MARCH 13

UNITED STATES OF AMERICA

"EVERYTHING AND EVERYONE HAS A STORY TO TELL. IT'S IMPORTANT THAT WE TAKE THE TIME TO SEE AND HEAR THAT STORY."
—JENNIFER TOWNE

ILLUSTRATION BY BRITNEY PHAN

KELLEE SANTIAGO

GAME DEVELOPER, PRODUCER, AND FOUNDER

Kellee sat in her computer chair, the light from the boxy monitor illuminating her face. She and her brother were playing *Sleuth*, a mystery game in which they had to solve a puzzle before time ran out. Behind her in the game, Kellee could hear footsteps. Her heart jumped into her throat as she raced to find the answer to the puzzle before her pursuer caught up with her.

Kellee adored games like this, games that were more than just shooting bad guys or finding the princess. She was always hunting for something that stood out.

While her friends in her theater group were happy to re-create famous Shakespeare scenes, Kellee would write new scripts in her notebooks. Role-playing games with high-fantasy backgrounds like *Final Fantasy* were popular, but Kellee didn't want to follow the trends. She focused on inventive ideas that were nothing like the games she had seen in store windows.

Overflowing with inspiration, Kellee decided to create her own gaming company. It gave Kellee the space to develop her own projects, like *Flower* and *Journey*. These games were groundbreaking, using music, flowers, and balls of light to tell the story. Even though the games had no words, they included images to help players feel strong emotions. You can play in a peaceful setting like an expansive field of flowers and still uncover unexpected adventures. That's exactly what Kellee wants—for players to be surprised by the unique worlds she creates.

Kellee continues to explore, allowing her creativity to blossom into new ideas that challenge how people experience gaming.

BORN 1979

VENEZUELA AND UNITED STATES OF AMERICA

"MY BIGGEST ACCOMPLISHMENT AS A DEVELOPER . . . HAS BEEN TO FORGE A SPACE FOR DEVELOPERS IN GAMES THAT EXPRESS EMOTIONS NOT TYPICALLY ASSOCIATED WITH TRADITIONAL VIDEO GAMES."
—KELLEE SANTIAGO

ILLUSTRATION BY
ANNA DIXON

MACKENSEIZE

STREAMER

Kenzie sat in the doctor's office, the paper on the table crackling under her hands. At 17, she had been imagining her life outside of high school, thinking about college, careers, and where she wanted to live. Now everything felt like it was crashing to a halt as the doctor explained that she had a type of seizure disorder called "epilepsy." The seizures, which caused her body to shake and her muscles to lock up, could happen at any time.

To control her seizures, Kenzie took medicine that made her feel tired. It was too dangerous for her to live alone. Suddenly her entire future seemed to be in peril, and there was nothing she could do about it. Hoping to find a way to distract herself, Kenzie began playing an online card game called *Hearthstone*. It turned out to be a perfect fit for her.

Wanting to meet more people who enjoyed it, she started YouTube and Twitch channels. She used the name Mackenseize as a nod to her disability. On her streams, she'd play her digital cards and explain her moves. Other players began watching and commenting on her videos.

However, as her community grew, Kenzie realized no one talked about disabilities like epilepsy. In fact, she wasn't sure she had ever seen another Twitch streamer with her disability. She decided she would share her experiences and create a space in her gaming community to help others understand disabilities like hers.

While she continues to experience the effects of her epilepsy, Kenzie uses her presence in the gaming community to openly talk about what she is going through. She encourages others to be patient with themselves, and never be ashamed of the challenges they may face.

BORN JUNE 8, 1992
UNITED STATES OF AMERICA

ILLUSTRATION BY
ANNA PERS BRÄCKE

"ONCE I START, I ALWAYS END
UP LOVING WHAT I'M DOING."
—MACKENSEIZE

MADDIE MESSER

GAMER

Maddie was lying on the sofa in the living room with her phone held above her. On the screen, she tapped frantically as her avatar swerved and jumped through obstacles in the game *Temple Run*. The farther she got, the faster her character ran, until she missed a jump and the game ended. As her score displayed, she sighed, looking with disappointment at her avatar. It was a boy.

Why don't the characters in my apps look like me? she wondered.

At 12 years old, Maddie loved playing app games on her phone. They were easy and fun, but she noticed that many of them didn't offer any female characters. Setting her phone down, she decided to conduct an experiment. She asked her parents if she could try a few more games.

The more games she downloaded and played, the more upset she became. Most of them didn't have female characters to play, and those that did often required her to pay real money to download them.

Maddie recorded her findings on a paper chart she'd made. Armed with her data, she wrote an article for the *Washington Post*, explaining that out of 50 games, only 46 percent of them offered female characters while 98 percent offered boy characters.

The creators of *Temple Run* saw Maddie's story. They developed a female character, finally allowing girl gamers to play as someone they identify with.

Maddie was pleased, but she knows it's not enough. She's become an advocate for adding better gender representation in games. She believes everyone should be able to see themselves on their screens.

BORN 2002

UNITED STATES OF AMERICA

"PROBLEMS GET FIXED WHEN PEOPLE DECIDE THAT THEY ARE TIRED OF WAITING AND DO SOMETHING."
—MADDIE MESSER

ILLUSTRATION BY MARLEN HACKER

MANAMI MATSUMAE

COMPOSER

SCAN TO HEAR MORE!

Once upon a time, a young girl in Japan counted out coins and dropped them into a purse before hurrying out of the house. She was on her way to the store to buy the newest album by a band from the UK called Queen. Manami loved music more than anything. She wanted to be like Queen and create music people around the world would listen to.

As Manami got older, she began playing games like *Super Mario* and *Dragon Quest* while studying piano. She liked the way video game music sounded. It was different from piano or guitar. The sounds were made on the computer, using programs to mimic the music of real instruments.

Manami applied for a job at a gaming company. She was shocked when she got the job—she'd never even used a computer before! Manami had no idea how she was going to change her piano music into something that would work for video games filled with pixelated heroes and monsters.

The first game Manami worked on was called *Mega Man*. The action game was about robots from the future. It needed a soundtrack, but it also needed sound effects for Mega Man's weapons and movements. Manami learned how to mimic footsteps on pavement and blaster sounds from guns. She plunked out notes on her piano and then translated them into a computer program. It made her think about each sound in a new way.

While Manami's music hasn't been played on tour by bands like Queen, it has still traveled around the world through each video game soundtrack. Her ability to adapt and be flexible has taken her on amazing journeys, showing her that there are always new ways to do something you love.

BORN DECEMBER 25, 1964
JAPAN

ILLUSTRATION BY
YADI LIU

"I LOOK AT THE ART
AND THE WORLD—
THE OVERALL IMAGE
THAT THEY'RE
GOING FOR—AND
THEN THE MUSIC JUST
COMES TO ME."
—MANAMI MATSUMAE

MARINA DÍEZ PEREIRO

GAME DEVELOPER

SCAN TO HEAR MORE!

Once upon a time, a deeply compassionate girl struggled to talk to her father. Sometimes he was sad, and sometimes he was happy. The changes happened in a way she didn't understand, and it made connecting with him difficult. To escape, Marina spent her time in role-playing video games. These adventures let her play as different characters in distant lands, far away from her struggles with her dad.

As Marina grew older, she realized games could do more than help her escape her personal challenges. They could also help her tell meaningful stories about those challenges.

Marina created the game *Hey, Dad: A Brief Story of a Mental Illness,* which explored her relationship with her father. Once the game was released, comments began to pour in from players who related to the story. Marina felt her heart squeeze as she realized how badly people needed to see mental health awareness in the world.

She started her own development team to make beautiful, creative games. In *Summer Gems,* two best friends explore the seaside, growing closer as they go on thrilling adventures. *Dordogne* uses unique watercolor animation to tell the story of a girl named Mimi as she reconnects with her childhood through puzzles from her grandmother. All of Marina's games are full of emotion, and she hopes they teach players new things about the world.

For Marina, it isn't enough to build games and promote them. She also travels the world to speak about the importance of diversity and mental health awareness. With each trip and each talk, she hopes to make the world a more accepting place—especially for those who are different.

BORN JUNE 3, 1994
SPAIN AND UNITED KINGDOM

ILLUSTRATION BY
INSU JO

"THE GAMES
INDUSTRY IS A
DIFFICULT PLACE,
BUT WORK HARD, LISTEN
TO ADVICE, TRUST YOUR GUT,
AND YOU WILL BE FINE."
—MARINA DÍEZ PEREIRO

MURIEL TRAMIS

GAME DESIGNER

Once upon a time, there was a clever girl who lived on Martinique, a small island in the Caribbean. Muriel loved to play board games, spending hours in the warm sunshine with friends and family. She was happiest when she was puzzling out exciting adventures or solving curious strategies on a game board.

When Muriel grew older, she left her home and family behind to go to school in Paris. While she enjoyed the challenges of learning engineering, she was homesick. She thought about her days playing games with the people she loved. Eventually, she decided to use her engineering skills for something new: a video game inspired by her childhood in the Caribbean.

Video games were different in the 1980s. They didn't have much detail, and characters were limited to simple movements and attacks. Muriel saw this as a challenge. She reimagined her childhood games as interactive, digital adventures, using pixelated art to create brightly illustrated settings. In her game *Freedom: Rebels in the Darkness,* Muriel told the story of four Black characters who were enslaved in the Caribbean in the 1800s. Her game *Urban Runner* is told as an interactive movie, in which players watch video clips and make choices to steer the story.

Muriel was the first Black female game designer. She worked with other men and women from Martinique, but also from the UK, Germany, Spain, and Romania. Their diverse backgrounds made the games stronger.

For Muriel, the best inspiration comes from the most familiar places. When she sees the pixelated images of the seashore on-screen, she's transported back to her days playing board games in the sun.

BORN SEPTEMBER 16, 1958
MARTINIQUE

PHOEBE WATSON

GAME DESIGNER

Once upon a time, a girl named Phoebe struggled to connect with her people and her culture. Her family always taught her to love her heritage as a woman of the Yarrer Gunditj Clan of the Maar Nation, a group of Indigenous people in Australia. But Phoebe still felt like she didn't belong. She lost herself in games like *The Sims 2* and the fantasy-adventure game *Skyrim*, avoiding how being different made her feel.

In college, Phoebe studied game design. She also became a cultural mentor, working with young Indigenous girls. These girls viewed their culture and heritage differently than she did. Phoebe was surprised—she hadn't expected to learn so much from the kids she was supposed to teach! She watched as their connections to their families and history helped them deal with bullying, friendship challenges, and school struggles. Phoebe began to think about what she was missing.

Empowered, Phoebe wondered if she could somehow translate her culture into her video games. She teamed up with DragonBear Studios, a game developer that celebrates diversity by adding Indigenous culture into games through stories and avatar appearances. She helped DragonBear show Indigenous characters accurately by portraying them in everyday clothes, not just ceremonial outfits.

Phoebe is only getting started as a game designer, but she is determined to create games that others can connect to and learn from. She hopes that Indigenous women around the world will be able to see themselves in the games they play, and that their cultures will be represented with respect.

BORN JANUARY 11, 1998
AUSTRALIA

"SINCE WORKING WITH
DRAGONBEAR STUDIOS,
I HAVE GROWN IN SO
MANY WAYS, BUT
IN PARTICULAR,
MY PRIDE FOR
MY CULTURE HAS
BLOSSOMED."
—PHOEBE WATSON

ILLUSTRATION BY
ANYA EVDOKIMOVA

POKIMANE

STREAMER

Once upon a time, a little girl in Canada fell in love with gaming while watching her brother play *Pokémon*. Imane sat, entranced, as beautiful worlds came to life on handheld screens and TV sets. With her controller in hand, she could dash across the screen as a Pokémon trainer or battle a warlock in *The Legend of Zelda*, unraveling amazing stories that stayed with her as she grew up.

Later, Imane switched from playing pixelated adventures on her bedroom floor to exploring online games with friends. When she was done playing, she would watch other girl gamers post their gaming adventures online. *I could do that too!* she thought.

Imane created a Twitch account called "Pokimane," a combination of her name and *Pokémon*, which ignited her love of gaming. As Pokimane, she streamed videos of herself playing *Fortnite* and *League of Legends*.

Imane's audience started out small, and she struggled to find her place on Twitch as a girl gamer. Sometimes, it was frustrating, but the more she played, the more her audience grew. One day, as she looked at the number of viewers watching her videos, she realized she could make streaming her full-time job. Maybe she could inspire other little girls to share their favorite games, as well.

Imane has become one of the most viewed female Twitch streamers online. Millions of people all over the world watch her videos. She hopes that when other girls see her streams, they'll understand there's a place for them in gaming too.

BORN MAY 14, 1996

CANADA AND MOROCCO

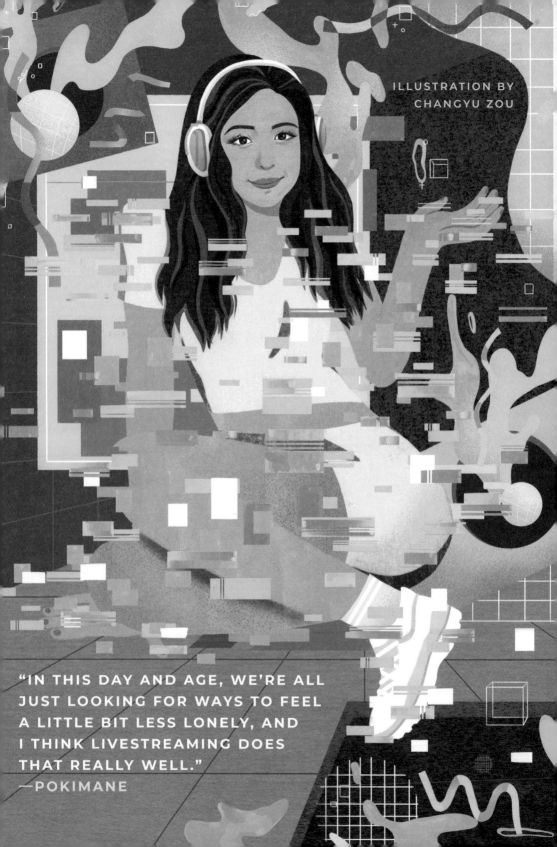

ILLUSTRATION BY
CHANGYU ZOU

"IN THIS DAY AND AGE, WE'RE ALL
JUST LOOKING FOR WAYS TO FEEL
A LITTLE BIT LESS LONELY, AND
I THINK LIVESTREAMING DOES
THAT REALLY WELL."
—POKIMANE

POORNIMA SEETHARAMAN

GAME DESIGNER

Poornima didn't notice the summer heat as she leaned over her friend's shoulder. On the computer before them, a patchwork of farms, buildings, rivers, and tiny people followed their every command as they took turns controlling the mouse. They were playing *Age of Empires II*, a game that let them create and conquer countries with their digital armies.

Poornima's favorite games let her build out her own worlds. She loved inventing new stories using the people, locations, and items in each game.

While she was passionate about gaming, Poornima had never considered a job as a video game designer. All the game developers she knew were men. It wasn't until a friend offered her a job as a video game programmer that Poornima realized her love of gaming could also be her career.

She learned that India, where she grew up and lived, was a perfect place to develop games for mobile phones. Not everybody had video game consoles, but lots of people had smartphones. They could play complicated adventures, like Poornima's childhood favorites, or simpler card or puzzle games.

Poornima began working with different mobile developers throughout India. She helped create a smartphone version of the horror adventure game *BioShock* and eventually moved on to help build games like *FarmVille 2: Country Escape*, which let players build and maintain farms filled with crops and animals on their computers or phones.

After years in the gaming industry, Poornima now decides how each video game is built and what it will look like. She's creating the world she wants to see—on-screen and off.

BORN JULY 18, 1984

INDIA

ILLUSTRATION BY
THUMY PHAN

"WE NEED MORE
FEMALE LEADERS
IN GAMING."
—POORNIMA
SEETHARAMAN

SASHA HOSTYN

ESPORTS PLAYER

SCAN TO HEAR MORE!

Sasha smiled as she lay on her bed rewatching the match. On the iPad screen, she was battling her opponent in *StarCraft II*. She knew that in just a few short moves, she would win. There were few women playing *StarCraft II* competitively, and every day Sasha seemed to be getting better, beating men who had been playing much longer than she had.

Even though she loved playing video games and loved competing even more, Sasha knew she needed to make a decision about college. Her father was a professor, and she didn't want to let her family down. But every time she sat down to work on college applications, her attention drifted to an upcoming *StarCraft II* competition called the Iron Lady.

She knew plenty of men in the esports community. They'd made playing in gaming competitions their careers! She decided that if she could win the Iron Lady, she might be able to do the same thing. She wouldn't have to study something she wasn't interested in. She just had to prove herself.

Competing wasn't easy. As a transgender girl, Sasha sometimes faced anger and intolerance from viewers and competitors. Some of the other women didn't think she should be allowed to compete. Sasha ignored them. She knew she was no different from any other player. Under the screen name Scarlett, she won match after match.

Sasha won the Iron Lady competition twice in a row. Instead of applying to college, she began competing all around the world. She's become one of the most successful women in the esports community. She is determined to prove that what matters most in a competition is hard work and dedication.

BORN DECEMBER 14, 1993
CANADA

ILLUSTRATION BY
MONTSE GALBANY

"IN TERMS OF ACTUAL PLAY,
THERE IS (AS FAR AS I KNOW)
NO ADVANTAGE TO BEING
BORN MALE OR FEMALE."
—SASHA HOSTYN

SHELLY MAZZANOBLE

GAMER AND PODCASTER

Shelly stared at the dice before looking up at the other people sitting at the table. She had been working for Wizards of the Coast, a company that builds tabletop fantasy games, for several years, but had never actually played one of their biggest games: *Dungeons & Dragons*.

I don't know about this, she said, but her friend running the game just smiled. Together, the group battled monsters, explored dungeons, and jumped over rivers to look for clues. Two hours later, Shelly was again looking at the dice she'd spent the night rolling in order to play her character—but with awe instead of doubt.

Shelly quickly realized that most *Dungeons & Dragons* players were men, but she thought that was ridiculous. Women have vibrant imaginations, and *D&D* was all about telling stories with friends. She knew she needed to get more women involved.

Shelly wrote a book called *Confessions of a Part-Time Sorceress: A Girl's Guide to the Dungeons and Dragons Game*. In it, she encouraged other women to try *D&D*, where a roll of the die can take you anywhere—into a hidden cave, across a rickety bridge, or to the highest tower in a castle. You can be an elf, a druid, a gnome, or anything you'd like. Your character's story is up to you! Shelly thought that was amazing.

Later, she helped start the official *D&D* podcast *Dragon Talk*, where she interviews players—including lots of women—about their experiences. Shelly wants women of all ages to embrace their inner wizards and fighters, and she can't wait to see what the next generation of *D&D* players will bring. She believes being yourself is the gateway to incredible adventures.

BORN FEBRUARY 1, 1972
UNITED STATES OF AMERICA

ILLUSTRATION BY
ELENA RESKO

"IF MORE WOMEN
ACTUALLY KNEW
WHAT THIS GAME
WAS REALLY ABOUT, I THINK
THEY WOULD BE INTO PLAYING."
—SHELLY MAZZANOBLE

SYLVIA GATHONI

ESPORTS PLAYER

When Sylvia's dad carried a PlayStation 2 into their living room in Kenya for the first time, Sylvia's world changed forever. She started playing *Tomb Raider*. Lara Croft, the main character, was strong and tough. Sylvia loved pretending she was Lara.

Between college classes, Sylvia played video games with friends. It was fun, but she wanted more of a challenge. When she heard about a video game tournament, she signed up. It was exciting to play in front of an audience, and she came in fourth. She signed up for another tournament. And another.

Eventually, Sylvia became the first female professional gamer in Kenya. She called herself QueenArrow, after one of her favorite comic book characters. She started playing all around the world. In 2018, Sylvia became the first Kenyan gamer to sign on to a professional esports team in the United States.

Still, some other gamers didn't take her seriously. *How can a young girl be a professional gamer?* they said.

I am a professional gamer, Sylvia said. *Not only that, but I'm going to be a lawyer at the same time.* She enrolled in law school. After graduation, she decided to use her knowledge of the law to protect her fellow esports players. Some laws in Kenya say that gaming and gambling are the same, and that gambling is bad. Sylvia wants to separate the two under the law so that gamers can keep playing.

And she uses her fame as QueenArrow to speak out for more diversity in gaming. When tournaments are advertised, Sylvia wants the marketing to include all types of people. One day soon, Sylvia hopes she won't be the only African woman sitting in the esports tournament chair.

BORN JULY 5, 1998
KENYA

ILLUSTRATION BY
DOMINIQUE RAMSEY

"ESPORTS IS FOR
ANYONE WITH
THE INTEREST
AND THE
DETERMINATION
TO SEE IT
THROUGH."
—SYLVIA GATHONI

WRITE YOUR STORY

_____

_____

_____

_____

_____

_____

_____

_____

_____

_____

_____

_____

_____

_____

_____

_____

DRAW YOUR PORTRAIT

KEEP PLAYING!

CREATE YOUR OWN CHARACTER

Game designers like Amy Hennig have brought rich and interesting characters to video games. Try your hand at designing your own.

1. Think about who you want your character to be. Do they live in a realistic world or a fantastical one? What do they look like? What are their traits? You can even be inspired by one of the people you've just read about.

2. On a sheet of paper, sketch out your character. Your drawing can be as detailed as you'd like.

3. Next to your character or on the other side of the page, list out some of your character's powers and attributes. What are they good at? What are their weaknesses? Do they have any special abilities? Think about what would make them a fun and interesting character to play in a video game.

4. Come up with a name for your character and write it at the top of the page. Maybe someday, they'll be the star of their own video game!

RESEARCH MODE

When Aya Kyogoku started working in video games, she was often the only woman on her team. Let's learn more about the people behind your favorite games.

1. Ask a grown-up's permission to do some online research.

2. Look up one of your favorite games. This could be something you play on a phone, a tablet, a game console, or a computer.

3. Look for a list of the people who worked on the game. If you're having trouble, try adding "credits" or "development team" after the name of the game in your search.
4. Find the name of a woman who worked on the game and look her up. See if you can find more information about her.
5. Write your own Rebel Girls story about the person you've found!

THEN AND NOW

Games have changed a lot over the years. When Muriel Tramis began designing video games, the visuals were very simple and the actions were limited. Find out more about what video games used to be like.

1. Find an adult you trust who played video games when they were younger. It could be your parent, an aunt or uncle, an older cousin, or a teacher.
2. Ask them some questions about what games they played growing up. Did they have a favorite? Where did they play it? What was it like to play?
3. Make a list of the similarities and differences between this game and one of your favorite games.
4. Together, predict what you think games will look like 10 years in the future. Write down your predictions. Maybe one day, when you are a grown-up, you will revisit them with a kid in your life.

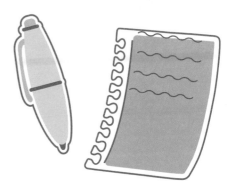

DECODE A MAZE

Developers like Marina Díez Pereiro use coding to make video games. Coding can be complicated, but it has simple building blocks that you can learn without a computer. Below, you'll see a code where each symbol represents a different direction. Using this code, make your way through the maze from start to finish.

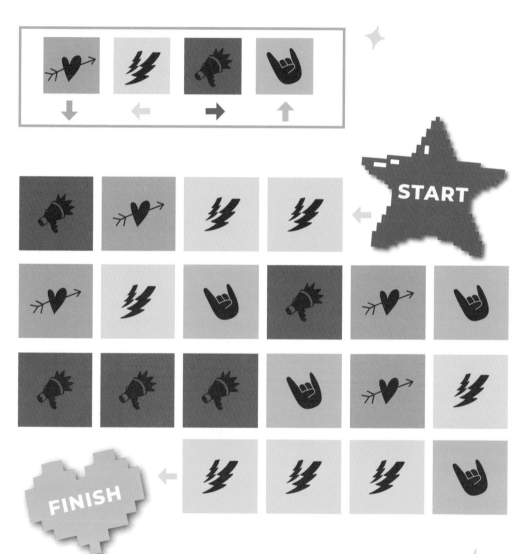

A NOTE ON ILLUSTRATIONS

In celebration of the incredible digital art found in video games, we explored some new types of art for this book.

The illustrations for Aya Kyogoku (page 14) and Jennifer Towne (page 30) were made in a 3D style. 3D illustrators use computer programs to design art that looks like it's coming right off the page. Some of these artists will even add animations, creating movement for their characters like video game designers do.

You may have noticed that two illustrations say, "Created using AI illustration." Take a look back at Amber Allen (page 6) and Amy Hennig (page 10). Our art director, Giulia Flamini, used AI, or artificial intelligence, software to make these works of art.

There are lots of different AI programs for creating images online. For some of them, you can upload a photo that you'd like your art to be based on. For others, you just need to type in descriptions. You can describe the subject you'd like to see, as well as the style, colors, and background elements. As a starting point for Amy's illustration, you might say something like: "Amy Hennig, sitting in a chair in front of big windows with space in the background in a pixelated video game style."

It often takes some tweaking to end up with an image you're satisfied with, and sometimes, AI doesn't quite get it right. While making these illustrations, we got some funny results, like people with too many fingers or shoes fused to their feet! Getting the perfect image can be a challenge, and it involves thinking creatively, putting in descriptive keywords, and picking the right inspiration photos. Behind each of these AI illustrations, there's still an element of human creativity.

We hope these illustrations make you think about all the incredible ways to make art. Grab your colored pencils, paints, clay, or computer and get creating!

For more stories about amazing women and girls, check out other Rebel Girls books.

LISTEN TO MORE EMPOWERING STORIES ON THE REBEL GIRLS APP!

Download the app to listen to beloved Rebel Girls stories, as well as brand-new tales of extraordinary women. Filled with the adventures and accomplishments of women from around the world and throughout history, the Rebel Girls app is designed to entertain, inspire, and build confidence in listeners everywhere.

THE ILLUSTRATORS

Twenty-three extraordinary female and nonbinary artists from all over the world illustrated the portraits in this book.

ANNA DIXON, USA, 33

ANNA PERS BRÄCKE, SWEDEN, 35

ANYA EVDOKIMOVA, UZBEKISTAN, 45

BEA BARROS, PHILIPPINES, 25

BRITNEY PHAN, USA, 31

CHANGYU ZOU, CHINA, 47

DOMINIQUE RAMSEY, USA, 55

ELENA RESKO, GERMANY, 53

GIULIA PIRAS, ITALY, 19

INSU JO, KOREA, 41

JULIETTE TOMA, USA, 23

KAITLIN JUNE, USA, 29

KATIE HICKS, CANADA, 13

KYLIE AKIA, USA, 43

LYDIA MBA, SPAIN, 17

MARCELA RODRIGUEZ, ARGENTINA, 15

MARLEN HACKER, GERMANY, 37

MONTSE GALBANY, SPAIN, 51

SHIRLEY HOTTIER, FRANCE, 9

SONIA LAZO, EL SALVADOR, 27

TALIA SKYLES, USA, 21

THUMY PHAN, VIETNAM, 49

YADI LIU, USA, 39

ABOUT REBEL GIRLS

REBEL GIRLS is a global, multi-platform empowerment brand dedicated to helping raise the most inspired and confident generation of girls through content, experiences, products, and community. Originating from an international best-selling children's book, Rebel Girls amplifies stories of real-life women throughout history, geography, and field of excellence. With a growing community of nearly 20 million self-identified Rebel Girls spanning more than 100 countries, the brand engages with Generation Alpha through its book series, award-winning podcast, events, and merchandise. With the 2021 launch of the Rebel Girls app, the company has created a flagship destination for girls to explore a wondrous world filled with inspiring true stories of extraordinary women.

As a B Corp, we're part of a global community of businesses that meets high standards.

Join the Rebel Girls community:
Facebook: facebook.com/rebelgirls
Instagram: @rebelgirls
Twitter: @rebelgirlsbook
TikTok: @rebelgirlsbook
Web: rebelgirls.com
Podcast: rebelgirls.com/podcast
App: rebelgirls.com/audio

If you liked this book, please take a moment to review it wherever you prefer!